HOW TO CREATE YOUR BUDGET

PERSONAL BUDGET

JELEEL TEMITOPE RAHEEM

ISBN: 9798363986420

DEDICATION

This book is dedicated to my late brother Abdullateef

CONTENTS

INTRODUCTION

How to create a personal budget You can get out of debt, make investments, and earn extra money regardless of your situation. Learn a way to create your budget today. Trouble making ends meet? Do you feel that money is not enough? Many believe that it is due to low income, but the harsh truth is that in the short term this is usually resolved by better managing the money that comes in. People always talk about how important it is to manage personal finances well, but that is not something that is taught in school. The most useful tool to better manage money (It does not matter if it is a little or a lot) is a personal budget, which allows you to see all the money that comes in and what it is spent on. Make one take control of your finances.

WHAT IS A PERSONAL BUDGET?

A budget is a document that shows all the money that comes in and goes out. It is a financial plan that revolves around a specific time and allows knowing the state of finances by classifying the accounts, taking into account fixed and extraordinary expenses and income.

So, a personal budget is one in which only personal income and expenses are shown.

The most common is to make a monthly personal budget since salary and other income are reported month by month, just as many expenses are measured monthly. Although depending on the income and objectives it can be done daily, weekly, fortnightly, or even annually.

For families with at least two sources of income and in which its members have various individual expenses but all depend on this income, it is best to make a family budget.

What is a personal budget for?

- Identify expendable or unnecessary expenses.
- Set financial goals.
- Plan the creation of a savings mattress or plan.
- Evaluate if you need to limit debts and credits.
- Create a spending or debt payment plan.
- Analyze if you need to generate more income.

These are some of the strengths of using this tool. It is recommended for everyone, but especially for those who have financial problems (or seek to avoid them) and those who have a goal that is achieved with money.

HOW TO CREATE A PERSONAL BUDGET

You already know what benefits the elaboration of a personal budget, so now it is time to talk about its elaboration. They are simple steps, but you need to pay attention.

The first thing to do is classify the accounts. That is, separate the money that comes in from the money that goes out and order it.

Then income and expenses are added separately.
With both categories totaled, subtract your expenses from your income.

Now it is that conclusions are drawn and decisions are made. The difference that remains determines whether you should cut expenses or shows your ability to save. If you want to "force yourself" to protect, include your savings in a spending category. This way you will always push yourself to keep.

Here are some examples of personal budgets in terms of income:

Most common income in a personal budget
The money that comes in is known as "revenue." Below we classify the most common income. Most people have at least one, which is their salary, although it all depends on the sources of income of each one:

- **Salary**: the money that comes from any job with an employer, even if you are the employer.

- **Scholarships**: if you are receiving scholarships or study aid, include them.

- **Rent**: money that comes from renting a property or other goods.

- **Fees**: if you are an independent professional and do not have a fixed salary (or it is a variable additional income).

- **Profit**: includes profits from a personal business.

- **Earnings**: If you make investments and generate profits regularly, include them in your income.

- **Pension and/or retirement**: includes the money that enters through private or social security plans.

- **Other income**: whether it is selling items regularly, receiving money for certain sporadic responsibilities, or possible government aid.

These categories are not set in stone and are just the most common forms of income. Include any source of money income, especially if it is recurring or secure.

Also, the correct thing to do is to record the net income, after taxes.

When the amount of income is not fixed, it is recommended to "punish the estimate". That is, put the lowest amount recently received.

income category	Amount
salary or salary	$25,000
Scholarship	$3,000
Money for bathing the dog	$3,500
Total revenue.	$31,500

Example of income in a personal budget
Most common expenses or expenses in personal budgets If you see that the amount of expenses is greater than the amount of income, do not be overwhelmed. Think that this is something completely normal because the monthly expenses of a person are varied.

The important thing is that when you subtract expenses from income, the number is positive and it is also significant for you.

Here are some of the most popular expense categories:

Accommodation costs

If you are paying rent, you should write down the expenses of this here.

If you are paying a mortgage, you should also list these expenses.

The cost of electricity. Being expenses that can change every month, it is best to look at how much you paid the previous year and make an average.

The payment of the water. As in the previous case, it is best to look at the average of what you spent previously.

House insurance costs.

Community expenses if any.

If you have a service at home, such as cleaning, you also have to write it down in the expense section.

Transportation expenses

The cost of loan debt. That is, the payments that you still have to face are included here.

The taxes are paid by your car.

The car insurance.

Fuel is a variable expense, but you can do a monthly average.

The costs of repairs and maintenance (such as oil changes or brake pads). To know what it costs you can call the mechanic and consult.

The cost of parking. Either in the car park next to your house or in other car parks. It is good that you make an average calculation of how much you will spend per month.

Car inspection is mandatory for older vehicles.

If you don't have a car, this category can be used for payments for any means of transportation you use.

Home spends

All food. We emphasize the word "everyone" as we also count candy, ice cream, or tacos.

The cost of lunch or coffee if you eat out.

All products are related to hygiene and beauty. They can be soap, shampoo, deodorant, toothpaste, and even makeup.

The clothes and the shoes.

The new furniture or appliances that you must buy.

Expenses related to pets and their care.

Other expenses that are usually fixed

Health insurance.

Children's expenses such as education and care (babysitting).

Mobile fee.

Gym subscription.

Payments of bank or financial loans.

Pension plan.

Entertainment (streaming services or cable TV, for example)

On the other hand, there are possible eventualities such as visits to the doctor, unplanned car repairs, and emergencies at home related to electricity, plumbing, and construction.

That's why it's important to follow money-saving tips that help you have an emergency fund separate from your savings.

Expense Categories	Amount
Food	$11,000
Transportation.	$4,000
Entertainment	$5,000
Total expenses	$20,000

Expense classification example

Personal budget example in theory you already know how to make a budget, because you know the classification of income and expenses.

However, it is really important to know the difference. That is the money that remains or is missing after making the budget. This way you will know what adjustments to make or you will be able to know the amount you can save each month.

HOW TO SET PERSONAL BUDGET GOALS

To stay motivated to follow your plan the best thing you can do is have a goal or objective.

There are many possibilities: get out of debt, increase savings to "X" amount, buy a car, accumulate capital, or invest. You decide the more specific and realistic you are, the better.

Mastering your budget should be one of your top goals if you're just starting to improve your finances.

From time to time look at your budget and analyze it to check if you are meeting your goals. You must do it often to know that you are on the right track.

To get what you want, it's best to set goals for yourself regularly. This way you will see how you improve over time.

Think short and long term. You can achieve some goals in a short time, but others, such as retirement plans, are long-term. You must take this into account.

Do not make a budget that is too tight, since it will most likely be too difficult to follow and in the end, you will end up leaving it. Being disciplined pays, but at the beginning, you can be flexible, there will be learning.

Tools to create and manage a personal budget
You already know how to prepare a personal budget, as you can see it is a meticulous task that requires some time.

The good news is that today there are various tools for finance. Here are the most outstanding:

Fintonic: This is an app to organize personal expenses quickly as it connects with various banks to avoid human errors. It is an app with multiple security measures and artificial intelligence that facilitates saving. Now it also offers immediate loans.

Pocketguard – This app can generate an overall budget automatically based on your spending habits, apart from other features.

Spendee – Thanks to this app, you will be able to track your expenses and your budget so that you can save more money. It is possible to connect the application to your bank account to keep track of all your expenses.

Key points when making a budget
Once the personal budget is made, you mustn't spend more money than you enter.

If you have many small expenses, instead of making a long list, make an "other" section. Pay special attention to this category.

In the end, you are the one who decides how you want to make the personal budget, so you do not have to strictly follow what I say in the article. The important thing is that you stay with the underlying idea.

FREQUENT QUESTIONS

What is income?
What are expenses?
Is a weekly personal budget a good idea?
Why not make an annual personal budget?
Tips for planning your budget
Keep all receipts so you can check your spending history.

Look at the expenses with a magnifying glass to know which ones you can do without.

Domicile payments to your accounts and cards to avoid default interest.

Always check your statements for possible errors, duplicate expenses, and the like.

Write down eventual expenses in the future and plan for them.

Have a cushion for unforeseen expenses.

Periodically review your budget to update amounts of expenses and income.

Take care not to include an expense or income several times

Set flexible and realistic limits.